Here Am I
Responding to God's Call

Anna Felix

HERE AM I
Responding to God's Call

Copyright © 2005 Anna Felix
Original edition published in English
under the title HERE AM I by
Kevin Mayhew Ltd, Buxhall, England.
This edition copyright © Fortress Press 2019

All rights reserved. Except for brief quotations
in critical articles or reviews, no part of this book
may be reproduced in any manner without
prior written permission from the publisher.
Email copyright@augsburgfortress.org or write
to Permissions, Fortress Press, PO Box 1209,
Minneapolis, MN 55440-1209.

Cover image: Cover photo by
Hydromet from iStock
Cover design: Emily Wyland

Print ISBN: 978-1-5064-5930-1

CONTENTS

Foreword	5
Introduction	7
1 Speak, Lord, Your Servant Is Listening: Samuel	9
2 Behold, the Servant of the Lord: Mary	31
3 Here Am I, Send Me: Isaiah	55
Epilogue	85

For Tim, who was called by God

FOREWORD

This book is about God. Yet it is solidly rooted in normal, everyday life. As we read, the veil between earth and heaven seems to grow thinner. The stories in Scripture connect and echo with our own stories. These biblical characters were real people, and their lives were touched and stirred by a real God. A child, a woman, and a man found God dealing with them, and they responded—and so may we.

Anna Felix has taken time with the Bible. This book owes much to her patient study. But she believes, too, that ordinary human experience is a holy "place." God values each person, and knows us so much better than we know ourselves. We only see the present; God sees the possibilities—all that we might become. This book will help readers to discover more of what God can do, in the ordinary, holy places where we spend our days.

There is material here to nourish personal faith, and ideas for local churches to take up. There are thoughts to savor, to pray over, and to turn into action. Enjoy this book. Learn from it. And grow in Christian faith and service.

REVEREND JOHN PROCTOR
Director of New Testament Studies
Westminster College, Cambridge

INTRODUCTION

This book is about personal encounter with God. It reflects on the experience of three great biblical characters: a child (Samuel), a woman (Mary), and a man (Isaiah). The chapters examine the pivotal, formative occasions on which they face up to the consequences of truly knowing the living God and affirm their own status before him. Each encounter is substantiated with some background relevant to the character's own life narrative, and the reader is invited to reflect how he or she might make the same response to God within his or her own story.

The chapters make reference to other parts of the Bible, reminding the reader that the Bible forms a whole story of salvation history. Themes and references recur throughout the Scriptures, and the hints in these chapters show how the significance of a text can be magnified by also considering its resonance in another chapter or book of the Bible.

The three chapter titles build a progression that the reader might recognize or aspire to in his or her own relationship with God. The progression builds from "I am listening" to "I am ready to obey" to "Send me." Each response is sufficient in itself but can be part of our ongoing conversation with God as we continue to get to know him through prayer, study, and good works.

The book sets out to encourage each reader and to validate the call of every child, woman, and man who seeks to know the Lord in person. It seeks to shed the light of Samuel, Mary, and Isaiah's experience on Christian life today and to suggest ways in which we might assimilate some aspects of their example into our own closer walk with God. The chapters conclude with questions for reflection and group discussion that draw on the "call experience" of the three characters. Some questions concern individual progress in living out the Christian life, and others concern the church community, inviting discussion on how your church could make the experience of God more accessible within the broad context of the chapter's themes.

The title of the book comes from the end dialogue of Isaiah's call. Isaiah hears the voice of the Lord say, "Whom shall I send and who will go for us?" And Isaiah replies, "Here am I, send me!" (see Isaiah 6:8).

1

SPEAK, LORD, YOUR SERVANT IS LISTENING: SAMUEL

In this chapter we reflect on the call of Samuel. You may wish to read the narrative in 1 Samuel 1–3.

BACKGROUND

Samuel was one of Israel's special babies, gifted by God to a woman who had not yet had a child in the normal course of her marriage. Samuel's mother Hannah was a beloved wife, the favorite of her husband's two wives, but taunted by her "rival" because she was unable to produce children.

Different translations of the Bible build the picture in different ways. The Jewish Publication Society (JPS) version of the *Tanakh*, which is the "standard Jewish Bible for the English-speaking world" shows us an authentic human family riven with the unhappy fall-out of competing relationships. When the family makes its yearly pilgrimage to Shiloh to sacrifice to God, the husband gives out the portions of the sacrifice according to the number of his dependants. Hannah receives one portion, and Peninnah, the other wife, receives one for herself and one for each of her children. This is Peninnah's once-a-year opportunity to shine. She is favored in front of the priests, other worshipers and God himself by the huge imbalance of sacrificial portions. The one thing she can surpass Hannah at—having children—is magnificently rewarded, and with every child she produces the gap between the women widens. Peninnah makes the most of this opportunity, and year after year she taunts Hannah until she cries and can't eat. Elkanah the husband tries to console Hannah with the reassurance that he is devoted to her, but this cannot change the ritual humiliation of the single portion and probably goads the jealous Peninnah (who covets equal affection and regard from her husband) into further teasing. Poor Hannah longs for just one child and one more portion of sacrifice to take the sting out of Peninnah's bitter triumph.

So much for the happy occasion of pilgrimage. The expedition should be the highlight of the year, but every year the reality is two unhappy wives, one revelling in spiteful delight at her yearly recognition and the other in the tears of ignominy. Elkanah does his duty and is utterly incompetent at making peace.

The Bible contains many stories of families that today would be called dysfunctional. We see blatant favoritism toward wives and children; we see rivalry between children of the same and of different mothers recurring throughout the narrative and leading inevitably to unhappiness and conflict. Better parenting, or better husbanding, according to the standards of the detached reader, might lead to happier lives, but the Bible deals in reality and normality. Very few families are perfectly functional; very few indeed operate without one or more members compensating for the intolerance or insecurity of other members.

The Bible never saves any embarrassment. It tells the truth about people as it brings to us the wonderful truth about God. God works with the righteous and the unrighteous, the happy and the unhappy, with good and bad alike. God works with our reality, whatever it is, transforming it lovingly toward his reality. Out of unhappy family life Hannah prayed to the Lord and proposed a bargain to him. She was to receive her request and an abundant overflow of generosity (in John 16:24, Jesus tells us: "Ask and you shall receive, so that your joy may be complete."

Hannah was bitterly unhappy. She cried a lot and neglected her health by not eating. Finally, one year at Shiloh, she left her meal uneaten and presented herself before the Lord to lay out her unhappiness before him and her proposition for his help. She fasted and prayed. Fasting makes the senses more alert and intentions more acute. It is recommended by Jesus for the serious cases of prayer as in the cure of the epileptic boy (Mark 9:29, in some versions and footnotes). Hannah's piety was not recognized by Eli the priest. She did not pray aloud in the conventional way; her lips were moving but she was praying in great and silent earnest with her spirit, and Eli thought she was drunk. He told her off for making a spectacle of herself, but when she explained, he blessed her with peace and added his "Amen" to her prayers (1 Samuel 1:17). After her prayers and Eli's blessing Hannah was happy. She ate and was glad and she left her petition confidently and patiently in God's hands. The NRSV says Hannah ate and drank with her husband, suggesting at last a proper feeling of celebration during the festal visit. In the JPS version "she ate and was no longer downcast." The omission of drink may suggest she was already preparing herself to carry a Nazirite child in her womb.

Hannah's bargain is interesting. She longed for a child to remove the disgrace of being barren. She asked for a child who would bring great honor to God through a life of more than usual devotion. The narrative clearly understands children to be God's gift. It says that the Lord had closed Hannah's womb. With hindsight perhaps the Lord closed her womb so that she should not be contented with normal efforts at motherhood but ask God for a specially devoted and holy child, and direct her mothering toward his service of the Lord. The dysfunctional situation of favoritism and counter-provocation lead to godly aspirations in Hannah and a resolution to lend back to God the greatest thing he could give to her—a child.

Hannah's response to her unhappiness was a measure of her goodness and sense of reality of God. Dysfunction does not lead of itself to holiness, but it can be a spur to a greater zeal in those who, like Hannah, recognize God's love as a real option in their sadness. The great good news of the Bible is that God brings great things out of misery and hopelessness when people ask him for his help.

Hannah asked specifically for a male child so that she could dedicate him to the strictest rule of life, that of the Nazirite, not as a temporary vow but until the day of his death. The angel who announced Samson's imminent conception to his unnamed and previously barren mother (Judges 13) gave instruction for Samson to live under that vow from conception. His mother had to refrain from wine, strong drink, and unclean food from that moment until after his birth. Who knows whether Hannah was thinking of Samson's mother when she made her promise and prepared herself for motherhood? The "Nazirite" means one who is separated or consecrated. John the Baptist appears to have lived under the same vow. His birth, too, was announced by an angel and his mother was previously barren. Samson, Samuel, and John were lifelong Nazirites with famous public ministries. In Jesus's time it was an honorable thing for those who could afford the elaborate and expensive ritual to take a temporary Nazirite vow lasting upward of thirty days. Under the vow they would fulfill some pledge or make an offering and be "holy unto the Lord." Vows were taken in the Temple's "Chamber of the Nazirites."

We have noted three special babies, all obvious gifts from God to barren women, all conceived in the due (if not overdue!) process of marriage. Of the mothers Hannah has a special place because she asked for her consecrated son. Her song, or prayer, when she left little Samuel with the Lord reads like a first draft of the Magnificat, which was said or sung by Mary (Luke 1:46–55), the mother of Jesus. Hannah continued to make a yearly pilgrimage to Shiloh and every year Eli would bless Elkanah and Hannah and ask God to grant them further children in place of Samuel who was lent to the Lord. God gave Hannah three more sons and two daughters, their God-given children to be the mother's happiness-at-home after the first had been given up in total consecration to God.

In some ways Samuel had the best of starts. He had a blessed birth. His mother gave him an early knowledge of the reality of God in her life. She placed him at Shiloh under Eli's care and tutelage where he could serve and come to know God in the most devoted way. Samuel did not appear to suffer any ill effects or dysfunction in his own life as a result of leaving home so early. His mother visited him and brought new clothes. Eli who looked after him was an experienced father; although his own sons had not turned out too well and, in due time, Samuel's sons also grow up to be disappointingly unholy. The reality of life is ever with us!

SAMUEL'S CALL

The text tells us that when God called Samuel, the word of the Lord was rare and visions were not widespread (1 Samuel 3:1). Among the people that you know there are probably few who would tell you of a personal encounter with God. Samuel knew about God and was enrolled in his service. He knew that he himself was God's gift to Hannah and had been dedicated to the Lord for his whole life. He had not yet had an encounter with God that would establish him in a personal relationship with him. He may not have had a concept of the Lord calling a person by name in order to give him a task. When the call came, Samuel was lying down in the temple (note the small t, it was a shrine or sanctuary at Shiloh) *where the ark of God was*. He was as close to God symbolically and sacramentally as it was possible to be.

The ark of God was a gold chest with carrying poles and angels at each end. It contained the tablets inscribed with the Ten Commandments, a pot of manna, and Aaron's rod that had sprouted. The flat lid of the chest was called the mercy seat and was metaphorically where God sat to dispense judgment (mercy). Unlike other judges God "sits" on the laws; he is not bound to observe the punishments laid down but has absolute freedom to dispense mercy. Sternness and mercy are both attributes of God but mercy is always thought to "cover" sternness. We can think about this when we button a shirt or coat: the underside with the buttons is God's guidance for our life, the topside with the buttonholes is God's forgiveness picking us up again and again. We are undone when we have lost track of either his guidance or his forgiveness or both!

When he heard his name, Samuel immediately assumed it was the familiar voice of Eli. God persisted in calling him through the period of his confusion, waiting patiently for the child to know his voice. When Eli realized God was calling Samuel he did not tell him to adopt an attitude of prayer or say a prayer or make an offering but told him to *lie down*, instructing him, *"if you are called again* say, 'Speak, Lord, for your servant is listening.'" Eli did not put fear or tension into the child. The encounter was absolutely normalized and all the initiative was left with God. The Lord called once more and Samuel answered as he had been taught. Samuel models for us the wonderfully uncomplicated response of an obedient child. He is dedicated to the Lord, why should the Lord not speak to him? Youth and inexperience do not disqualify anyone from receiving God's word. Children hear God speaking as naturally as they hear their parents. God's business with Samuel was to denounce Eli's sons in strong and unambiguous terms. Samuel was afraid to tell the priest, but he probably didn't know that Eli already had the gossip on his sons from the local inhabitants and that a "man of God" had already delivered a similar denouncement (1 Samuel 2:27–36).

It is a tradition of the Scriptures that "by the evidence of two or three witnesses a thing is established." The twofold delivery of the message to Eli establishes its truth beyond doubt—and authenticates Samuel's commission. In Deuteronomy 19:15 and 2 Corinthians 13:1 this applies to crimes; in John's Gospel (8:17) Jesus explicitly applies the principle to evidence about himself and John uses the method in several places—for example, in John 4:42 Samaritans agree with the woman from the well that Jesus is truly the Savior of the world; in 5:31–38 John the Baptist, the collected miracles, and the Father testify to Jesus. John picks up the theme again in his letter, in 1 John 5:7–8: "There are three that testify: the Spirit and the water and the blood, and these three agree." Matthew also seems to like the principle, where Mark has one blind man cured, Matthew has two! (See Mark 10:46–52 and Matthew 9:27–34.) Even the body and blood of the sacrament may be two witnesses to establish that Jesus is truly present. The body represents Jesus's self (compare the words "some*one*" and "some*body*"), and the blood represents his life. Jesus's self and life witness to the same presence.

REFLECTIONS FOR OUR OWN DISCIPLEHOOD

1. Touching base with Samuel

Samuel was a special child in having the preparation and opportunity to hear God calling him. Praying with children, reading the Bible with them, and taking (not sending!) them to church all nurture an unforced love for God in preparation for his self-revelation at a time of his choosing. Children will love God without questioning his existence, but they need to be taught that his presence can be felt and known with the same certainty and comfort that we can feel the presence of people in another room at home. They should not grow up thinking that worship is speaking into a void without affirmation that the worship is heard; that would be the road to falling away from faith and prayer. They should be assured that God hears us and sometimes lets us feel the holiness of heaven around us as we pray. When adult worshipers say, "Wasn't that beautiful?" they sometimes mean, "Did you feel the presence of God?"

As an attendant in the temple, Samuel wore a linen *ephod*, a tabard-like over-garment for the upper body worn by priests and others engaged in holy duties. His attire, like a server's robe, reminded him that he was in the holy place as a person dedicated to God. Wearing a cross, a crucifix, or a holy medallion can be a similar personal reminder to us during our everyday life.

Samuel was as close to the presence of God as it was possible to be. When we pray in front of the reserved sacrament, we are in the presence of God. The tabernacle is also an ark (a place of safekeeping) containing the teaching of God, this time as Jesus, the living Word of God, under the outward form of consecrated bread. When we pray in any place where we habitually make time to be with God (this could be our bedside) or in a place where others have prayed and established a tradition of holiness of place (this could be a church or a place of pilgrimage) we are like Samuel in a place set apart for God to be heard as well as spoken to. It is also true that God chooses his place and his moment, but we are concerned here with the time we make ourselves available for listening, the time that demonstrates our conviction that communication with God is real and not superficial or rushed. Sometimes in prayer we might strain our senses to feel God's presence or hear his voice within us, or be aware of a conviction of his will rising inside us, but Samuel gives us a model of restful openness, of being available to God but not disappointed if he does not choose this moment to speak.

Samuel grew up to be a seer (see-er, one who "sees" God) and a prophet (one who speaks for God). He continued to be in close personal contact with God throughout his life. Our sense of God's presence may be overwhelming only at times in our life. This does not mean he is absent at other times or before we feel his presence for the first time. That feeling of his presence is his gift and it is his to bestow and to withdraw. Sometimes it is good for our growth in faith and trust not to feel him for a time; then we learn to know he is there without the evidence of our feelings. These are also times to reinforce that it is God we love, not the feeling of God. The highlights of our prayer time reassure us of the reality and effectiveness of more mundane occasions. If we stop short at trying to summon or recreate feelings of God-with-us we are not aiming our prayers at heaven, but at ourselves. We can be comforted in knowing God is real; he is with us and he loves us. If we are open to him and *if he calls us*, then we know what to say!

God's word to Samuel was a difficult message for a child to hear in his first meeting with his Lord, and here our experience is likely to diverge from Samuel's. Our first certainties of God's presence are much more likely to feature Jesus's themes of love, restoration, healing, and forgiveness. This is most likely, but not necessarily the case. The children who saw visions of Our Lady at Fatima were shown terrible aspects of human behavior and God's justice and were given a burden of prayer for repentance. We must remain aware that it is a fearsome and serious business to fall into the hands of the living God. Fearsome does not mean frightening and we should remember that angels usually begin their message by saying, "Do not be afraid."

The message that Samuel received is unexpected in the build up of the story. We might have anticipated God would announce Samuel's special ministry to him. Instead the child was given the awkward and damning message about his guardian's sons. The message was specific and personal to the moment; although of course it carries a general warning to be true to one's commission. What is generally drawn out, and what is most relevant to us, is Samuel learning in his youth to listen to his absolutely real and present God. The story gives us "double witnesses" so that we should know the account is trustworthy. Hannah's answered prayer and Samuel's subsequent career as a prophet are double witnesses to personal relationship with God. The Nazirite vow and living in the temple are special features of Samuel's story bearing witness to his special career.

Our story will have its own special features, promises, and encounters. We can "touch base" with Samuel by being faithful in our prayers and living a life that serves God even before we have personal affirmation of the truth and reality of God. As they were for Samuel, the faith and the answered prayers of others and the long tradition of worship are our evidence of God whom we will one day know "face to face." Like Samuel, we can be available to God in quiet time. Perhaps we can be under the tutelage or example of priests and religious people, in our parish or on retreats, as Samuel was under the tutelage of Eli. We should learn to "wait upon God" so that we expect to feel his presence and hear his inward voice. Even when we have prayed for the Lord to reveal his presence to us, we can be overcome by the gravity and awe of the experience; we should remember the words that anticipate and hush our holy fear, "Do not be afraid."

Samuel models for us the progress between knowing about God and knowing God. In his case God's self-revelation was unexpected: he was unfamiliar with the concept of God speaking with individuals. We are able to anticipate and look forward to the Lord making himself known to us in a personal way. We should recognize his presence and not be afraid because it is an experience we pray for, confident that God also longs for us to cleave closer to him.

2. Paving the way and sharing the message

Samuel's caregiver, Eli, had not prepared the young boy for a personal encounter. He himself was probably not expecting Samuel to encounter the Lord for many years to come, but in the middle of the night he was awake to the source of the repeated calling. This offers two lessons to parents and caregivers. First, that we should teach our young that relationship with God is personal so that they expect and recognize him when he allows them to feel his presence or has a message for them. Second, that we should talk to our children about the experience of faith, normalizing the idea of "knowing God" and encouraging them to share their experience with us. This is important so that we can affirm them in their encounter and empower them to reflect on its significance in their life and faith. A child should rejoice in their personal knowledge of God rather than suppress it through fear, or misinterpretation, or the impression that something strange, even freaky, has happened to them. Fifty percent of adults report having had a "spiritual experience" in their lives, but many do not attribute it to God or seek to assimilate it into their whole "life event." They regard it as an oddity, unexplained and therefore better left alone.

The question of speaking to a wider audience about our faith is delicate. I knew a Christian timeshare salesman who, it was said, would spend two hours talking about Jesus and one hour talking about the timeshare. He had the highest sales record in the company, but the trainees who sat in with him were at a loss as to how to repeat the trick themselves. He was one of those gifted people who could talk to anyone about Christianity—even when they had a specific appointment to talk about something else—and have them completely on his side whether they were believers or not. Most of us, I would venture, find it daunting enough to talk to fellow churchgoers about our faith, let alone neighbors, friends, colleagues or strangers.

The prophets were *required* to announce "Thus says the Lord" when they were commissioned by him to bear messages. The *Shema* (Deuteronomy 6:4–9) is the passage that Jews recite on waking and retiring; it is the last thing they say or hear when they die. "*Shema*, Israel" are the opening words and mean "Hear (and obey), O Israel." Since it is such a significant passage and we will refer to it again, included below is a rendering taken from a book of Jewish prayers and based on the NIV translation:

> *Hear O Israel,*
> *the Lord our God,*
> *the Lord is one.*

> *Love the Lord your God*
> *with all your heart and with all your soul*
> *and with all your strength.*
> *These commandments that I give you today*
> *are to lie upon your hearts.*
> *Impress them on your children:*
> *talk about them when you sit at home*
> *and when you walk along the road,*
> *when you lie down and when you get up.*
> *Tie them as symbols*
> *on your hands, that they may do good,*
> *and on your foreheads,*
> *that your eyes may see and have mercy.*
> *Write them on the doorframes of your houses*
> *and on the gates of the city,*
> *as a reminder that it is the dwelling place*
> *of the Eternal God.**

The passage prescribes talking about God's commandments at every opportunity. This amounts to talking about a life that is lived as close to the Lord as possible. It conveys a sense of taking delight in the Lord so that it is a joy to discuss his teachings, to do good and have mercy and remember that God lives among us. Direct experience of God would seem to belong to this same discussion and be appropriate everyday (or ordinary) conversation between believers.

At the end of the Gospel (Matthew 28:19) Jesus sends his disciples to tell the good news to the world; this may also be translated as, *"As you go on your way through the world, make disciples . . ."* Sometimes Jesus tells individuals to spread the word of their encounter

---

* *Praying with the Jewish Tradition* (Triangle Books, 1988).

with him (e.g. the cured, Gentile demoniac from Gerasene at Mark 5:19), yet, at other times, he orders people to keep their experience to themselves—for example, the cured deaf man (Mark 7:36). And in this way Mary treasured events in her heart rather than broadcasting them (Luke 2:19 and 51). We can interpret the "messianic secret" as belonging only to the lifetime of Jesus of Nazareth, lest the reports of miracles interfered with the progress of his mission. After his death and resurrection there is no such secret. The news of his rising when all seemed lost is so amazing no one can keep it to themselves. The same joy in telling should be ours. Perhaps we need to ponder the amazing truth we believe until it strikes us anew how fantastic and how "tellable" it is.

When Jesus sent out disciples to "warm up" towns for his own teaching visits, he advised them not to persist with their message where people didn't want to hear it (Luke 9:5) but to move on to other audiences. Jesus was concerned that there was too little time available to waste on the unwilling; nevertheless the advice has value for us today. The teaching not to give what is holy to dogs or cast our pearls before swine (Matthew 7:6) gives us a clue to Jesus's caution on our behalf. We should be careful how we expose our faith experience to those who are unsympathetic or hostile or liable to deride it. The experience is very precious to us; it moves us at the level of the soul and it is at the same deep level that we are open to damage if our story is not respected. It would seem safe and appropriate to share with our fellow believers and with seekers who will be affirmed by our experience.

In summary, it is right and proper and a natural outcome of belief to share the gospel with others. This includes our experience of God since it is relationship that makes the story real to us and to others. It is appropriate to share with unbelievers and even with skeptics (or else how will we promote the gospel?), but this is probably best done within a previously defined context where faith sharing is on the agenda, or at the level of friendship that accommodates other topics for sharing, so why not also the experience of God? In these circumstances our sharings can find a congenial context and the listener is better disposed to hear us openly rather than defensively, fearing an aggressive conversion motive. The knee-jerk reaction to such a fear is for the swine to trample the pearls and turn to gore the caster of the treasures.

Talking to our children of any age should never fall within the category of pearls before swine. And however resistant they have grown to faith out of peer pressure or loss of habit we should continue to maintain it as a normal topic of conversation, gently persisting in declaring the reality of God's presence. When our children know their need of faith they will be able to take it first on our authority (if they have no childhood experience to refer to) and be assured that God's own affirmation of his love for them is an experience that is open to them.

3. The single life and family life

Samuel also models for us the single life, lived close to God. He served in the temple by day and slept in God's presence by night. At the time of his call, Samuel had no dependants and no obligations of care; he was utterly free to attend upon God. In our different contexts of school, work, and retirement there are material calls on our time—jobs to be done, people to engage with—yet we can maintain a closeness to God by thinking of him often, offering up quick prayers (even just "Lord") that punctuate our awareness of how we think, speak, and act. When the single life gives way to responsibilities of spouse and children, the demands upon our time multiply, yet it remains possible to keep glancing at God, to keep in touch, to allow our mind to return to him often. This keeps us open to God, and keeps us mindful of his presence so that we do not fall away from faith through busyness. If we think of God often and keep the relationship alive, then Sunday worship, for example, will remain a priority and not cede to being a competing activity with children's football or swimming lessons. It is only relationship with God and not habit alone that can withstand the pressure to allow Sunday to be just another Saturday.

Our frequent reference to God could be likened to looking in the rearview mirror of the car every five seconds as our instructor taught us. The constant glancing away from the road in front does not impair our driving but adds to our safety and awareness along the journey. Thoughts of God are not of course looking backward, but give us a bigger awareness in what would otherwise be a limited field of vision.

Constantly darting our thoughts to God echoes the final urging of the *Shema*, to remember that "the city" is the dwelling place of God. Would we not live differently if we were constantly aware of having God as our neighbor, of sharing our living space with him? In Christian terms we think of Jesus as our neighbor. *The Message* translation of John's Prologue tells us "[The Word of God] moved into the neighborhood" (John 1:14). This is not intended to scare us into good behaviour but to make us rejoice that he is not remote but near at hand. It is evidence of his love that he chooses to be near us: he is not the headmaster patrolling the corridors with his cane! Our mental picture of Jesus living among us should be the tableau that drew thousands of families to listen to him in his lifetime: Jesus seated, talking of the generosity and justice to be found in the kingdom of God. The man and his teaching are so compelling that we also feel inspired to be part of that kingdom, to assist in actualizing the prayer "Thy kingdom come." Wherever he was, in the countryside, the towns, or in people's homes, the crowds tried to come close to him, to listen to him and have their infirmities healed by him.

4. Children of God

Jesus praised the qualities of childhood that render little people more open to God's kingdom than their cynical, world-weary parents. He said we have to accept the kingdom like a child or we will never enter it (Mark 10:15). Children find it easy to believe things that are lovely and are told them by people who care about them. They hear the stories of Jesus joyfully without worrying about what others will say and without looking for an explanation to debunk his miracles or dumb down his demands. If he is the Son of God why would he not feed and heal and raise from the dead? What is hard about any of that for God? Children are the center of their parents' lives. It makes absolute sense to them to be special to Jesus: why would he not love them too? It is perhaps teaching about forgiveness that adults particularly need to accept with the simplicity of a child, remembering how easily they forgive little children without counting the cost, because the children "know not what they do" (Luke 23:34).

Samuel was a special child, God's answer to his mother's prayer. She placed him close to God where he heard the voice of the Lord for himself. Let us strive to wait upon God as Samuel did, and to bring our children into his presence as Hannah had done, for we have the promise of John's Gospel (1:12), "To all who did accept him he gave power to become the children of God."

Questions for reflection or group discussion

1. (a) Were you ever taught to listen for God's call? Do you teach/have you taught your children to listen for God's promptings and call?

   (b) How often do you set aside time for "listening to God" or "waiting upon him"? (This could be time you call "adoration" or "meditation.") Share your experiences of "hearing God's voice." This could be, for example, a growing or sudden conviction of a right course of action when you have been anxious or praying about something; a soothing of worries with a sense that God is in control and all will be well; a Bible text that was particularly apt or that you suddenly understood as God's word to you personally.

2. (a) Does your church building convey a sense of God-with-us when you enter it? Share your experiences of feeling his presence.

   (b) What could you do to make your building "speak louder" of the presence of God so that people expect to find him there and can easily open themselves to his presence?

3. (a) Does the teaching in your church move people on from knowing *about* God to the expectation and experience of knowing God?

   (b) What can your church do to welcome children and assist them to personal encounter with God?

Additional Bible readings concerning the births of other special babies

- Samson, born to be a Nazirite and to deliver Israel from the Philistines. In Judges 13, notice how Manoah and his wife do not expect to see God and survive. Reflect on how the incarnation of Jesus renders seeing God survivable and an experience for all.
- John the Baptist, born to be a Nazirite and the forerunner of the Lord, possessed by the spirit and power of Elijah. In Luke 1:5–25, notice how Elizabeth, like Hannah, suffered "reproach among men" because she was barren. Reflect on how God overturns such reproach with huge recompense.
- Jesus, the Son of God—Matthew 1:18–25.

Summary of key themes

- Some children are called into life for God's service.
- God works with our reality—happy or unhappy—to further his kingdom, if only we offer ourselves in his service.
- The heart of our religion is "knowing the Lord." All of our worship, study, and good works should be undertaken in the desire to know him more intimately.

Take-home message to think and pray about

- We need to "stay close" to God to be available to him and hear his promptings. How can we integrate God into every hour of our lives?

Prayer projects
- Pray for opportunities to reach children in your parish.
- Pray that children and their parents/guardians will come into a relationship with God that transcends the view of "church" as "an activity," "tradition," or "not for us."

Prayer
Speak, Lord, your servant is listening.
Lord, keep me close to you
when I am awake and when I am sleeping.
Keep calling me and help me answer,
"Here am I, send me."
Amen.

2

BEHOLD, THE SERVANT OF THE LORD: MARY

*This chapter discusses Mary.
You may like to read Luke 1:26–55.*

BACKGROUND

Mary was a young, unmarried woman. Since she was unmarried she was perhaps as young as thirteen or fourteen, just entering childbearing, and therefore marriageable, age. Although life expectancy was set by the psalmist at seventy years or eighty "if we have strength" (Psalm 90:10), illnesses, injuries, and childbirth would have carried off many at a much younger age. Childhood was short and we must consider Mary to be a woman, not a child. Mary is often celebrated for her ordinariness, her place as a representative woman, but some traditions both younger and ancient disagree with this.

Michelangelo began the tradition that Mary did not age by sculpting her as a beautiful young woman no older than her son in his *Pieta*. To accord her youth and beauty was to pay tribute to her "Yes" to God that gained the salvation of all Christians. It is also to express the radiant beauty of a life lived in obedience to God, accepting from him both joy and sorrow, clarity and confusion, knowing that he does not think as people think, that a day in his courts is better than a thousand here, and that ultimately all shall be well. Such a life is rare, and it would not be surprising if Mary had been trained for her life of trust and obedience.

The tradition that Mary had an immaculate conception is that she was the natural child of her parents Anne and Joachim, yet began her life without acquiring "original sin" from her parents. Such a birth describes the rarity of a person who could bear the danger, the glory, and the sorrow of mothering the Son of God. Another tradition has Mary raised in the Temple. We should expect that she would be well educated, well versed in the tradition and practice of her faith. Jesus was not dedicated to service in the Temple like Samuel. He was raised at home, away from the danger, intrigue, and accessibility to enemies that he might suffer after his notable and auspicious birth! Without original sin that baulks at God's authority, Mary would be able to accept the responsibility for the tiny godhead in her care, and to allow the rejection, hatred, and willful misunderstanding he later suffered to be the will of God. She could not expect him to lead an average kind of family life and had to accept that God his Father would have his prior love and obedience. Only a special mother could cope with this ultimate reconstituted family and the ultimate love and trust (and pain) required every time she let her son go into his Father's care or about his Father's business.

An extraordinary woman must have had an extraordinary husband. Young people are sometimes horrified to hear that Joseph may have been around forty-two at the time of the marriage. Men sometimes deferred marriage from the age of twenty-one or so in blocks of seven years to study, some marrying at twenty-eight or thirty-five. Since family life is a given in Judaism, men are not celibate for the sake of God, and Joseph at forty-two would have completed the maximum extended study period, the maximum preparation to help raise such a precious child. It takes a mature kind of man to raise another man's child, and we should be sympathetic with Joseph requiring his own visit from an angel (Matthew 1:18–23), as Samson's father had done (Judges 13:8–23) when his child was announced even though he, Manoah, was to be the father.

When we consider "special babies" in the Bible, conception by an unmarried woman and a barren wife are comparable in being manifestly due to God's intervention. Where the mother is unmarried, the father must be God since there is no husband and we have the ultimate "special baby." Joseph took special care of Jesus, ensuring everything was done for him that Hebrew teaching required, that he was safe from the murderous Herod, and that he attended the pilgrim feasts in Jerusalem after Herod's death. "All Israel" (literally every male over thirteen) was required to present himself before the Lord three times a year at the feasts of Passover, Pentecost, and Tabernacles. Families living in rural places and provincial towns would probably not have been able to afford to leave home and be absent from work three times a year to walk to Jerusalem, spend several days encamped at the Temple or with friends for the festal observances, and walk home again. It would appear that Joseph ensured his family did make the pilgrimages during Jesus's young childhood and into his adult life. Probably he could obtain carpenter's work along the journey and in Jerusalem to support them while they were away from home.

When Jesus was twelve or thirteen he would have become *Bar Mitzvah*, son of the commandment, probably in a ceremony during the family's Passover visit to the Temple. Unknown to Mary and Joseph he stayed behind when they began the homeward journey. He was independent in the Temple for five days—the two days Mary and Joseph spent traveling homeward and back again, and the three days they spent searching Jerusalem. The young man Jesus impressed the teachers in the Temple with his understanding and his answers. He rebuked poor Mary for worrying and not anticipating he would be about his Father's business. When Jesus became *Bar Mitzvah*, Joseph, like other fathers, was released from responsibility for his boy's religious observance. It was becoming apparent to both Mary and Joseph that their role was changing and that Jesus's real Father would have increasing influence in his life. Nevertheless, although their little boy was now technically a man, he returned to Nazareth and was obedient to them. "And Jesus increased in wisdom and in stature and in favor with God and people" (Luke 2:52). This appendage to the incident is very like a verse about Samuel inserted between the account of Eli's sons' behavior and their denouncement by the "man of God." It reads, "Now the boy Samuel continued to grow both in stature and in favor with the Lord and with the people" (1 Samuel 2:26). Samuel was growing up in the temple; John's Gospel teaches that Jesus is the real Temple; the real interface between God and people. In his young manhood he was growing in favor with both.

Mary had a special start in life. Tradition also gives her a special end describing her "dormition" and "assumption into heaven." A very few, very special biblical characters did not die in the conventional sense. One of these was Enoch: "Enoch walked with

God; then he was no more, because God took him" (Genesis 5:24). We know very little else about Enoch. He was the son of Jared and the father of Methuselah and had other sons and daughters; he lived to be three hundred and sixty-five years old (possibly according to a different system of counting years!). It is a marvellous description of a life that someone walked with God. Enoch walked so closely with God that he could pass into God's nearer presence without shedding the encumbrance of his body.

Elijah the Tishbite also escaped death. He was taken up into a whirlwind (2 Kings 2:11). In Elijah's case the tradition persisted that since he had not died he would return. At the end of Malachi 4:5–6, he is prophesied as a reconciler of families. In Mark 9:13, Jesus suggests that Elijah did return in the person of John the Baptist and was put to death. Jews today still anticipate Elijah's return: a cup of wine is filled for him at the Passover meal and the door is opened for him to come in. Sometimes when a disagreement cannot be resolved, they may agree to "wait until the Tishbite comes" because he will settle all disputes.

Mary's dormition is her final falling asleep after which Catholic tradition has her assumed (taken) body and soul into heaven, where she is crowned queen. Mary's stature as queen mother in heaven is comparable with that of her counterparts in European kingdoms a few hundred years ago. She has authority, status, and reverence on account of her son. She has influence over her son especially in situations of asking him to show mercy. In earthly terms if you did not succeed with the king, there was only one person to whom you might attempt going, "over his head" and that would be his mother, to whom he was once obedient as a child, and from whom he learned gentleness and courtesy, while he learned courage, responsibility, and the necessary art of war from his late father. The queen mother was a national treasure on account of having produced and raised the king in whose hands the lives and prosperity of his subjects were held. In times when kingdoms stood and fell by the strength of their king, a good king was the savior of his people and his mother, the source of their salvation. Some Christian traditions are not comfortable with calling Mary "Queen of Heaven" or "Mother of God" or using other Catholic and Orthodox titles; yet even if we call her "Mary of Nazareth," the label instantly conveys a status of association with her son, whom Pilate advertised as "Jesus of Nazareth, King of the Jews."

MARY'S CALL

When the angel came to Mary, her future lay unknown before her. The angel gave her the customary reassurance, "Do not be afraid," and blessed her. He then told her what would happen. Mary did not complain or excuse herself but asked the practical question, "How can this be?" and got a practical answer: "The power of the Most High will overshadow you." And then she responded, "Behold, the handmaid of the Lord, let it be to me as you have said." She gave her agreement, her Amen to God.

Mary's call is an extreme case of the disturbance a religious experience can cause in a person's life! Seeking sympathetic female company she went "in haste" to stay with her miraculously pregnant cousin Elizabeth. Elizabeth was at last bearing her husband Zechariah's child, although he was still dumbstruck after doubting the angel who gave him the good news (see Luke 1:5–25). Elizabeth would understand the turmoil of Mary's blessing and so Mary stayed with her for three months, giving Joseph space to come to terms with things while her body taught her the physical truth that she was having a child. On her arrival at Elizabeth's, Mary was blessed with confirmation of her condition. John the Baptist leapt in his mother's womb and Elizabeth proclaimed her mother of the Lord. Mary praised God in poetry (the Magnificat—see Luke 1:46–55) that echoed the song of Hannah. She celebrated with Elizabeth the power of God to give life, to reverse fortunes, and to show both justice and mercy.

Mary knew the gist of her vocation: she was to be the mother of the King of Israel and Son of God without the intervention of a man. Her role and her pain unfolded as time went by. She loved her son through the spectrum of experience from worship by angels, shepherds, and wise men, through to the six hours of his crucifixion and laying him in a tomb. The story was neither as one would expect nor plan from the birth in a stable to the burial in a (temporarily) borrowed tomb. Jesus's kingship was obvious to some, from the Magi to Pilate, yet on the same evidence it was obscure to others. His power was obviously godly and life-giving to some and, on the same evidence, suspicious and threatening to others.

In her motherhood, Mary's love was so perfectly, unreservedly given to her son that it became inseparable from the love within him, and so we can truly believe that she loves each one of us as her child. As a mother she protected her infant son from danger, but as he grew she did not protect him from his vocation. When Jesus said to her from the cross, "Look at your son" (John 19:26) it is usually taken to mean, "Look at John." We can also, at least for a moment, think of him saying, "Look at me. Look at the great victory your son is accomplishing. Don't think this is a disaster; I was born for this." As soon as he says, "Look at your mother" we are back with the traditional interpretation of Jesus taking care of his mother, and entrusting all Christians to her love.

One of the strongest features of Mary's motherhood is allowing God the Father full access to his Son. A mother would deter her son from a face-off with the devil, but Mary's son, filled with his Father's Spirit, answered the temptations of the devil by quoting the word of God and the Scriptures, until the devil gave up and left him. Mary could not go to comfort her son in the desert after his ordeal, but his Father sent his angels. In our little way we know we cannot go to our young son when he falls on the football pitch but have to leave him to the coach who will usually get him up with a few brisk words and a splash of cold water. Most mothers prefer their sons not to mix with those at the dangerous margins of society, the contagious, the criminal, the socially and politically unsavory. Mary's son, filled with his Father's Spirit, could not be contaminated by sickness or immorality but soothed and reintegrated those rejected people. While the Son of God is a special case regarding what he can do and where he can safely go (he always knew he would only die in Jerusalem, publicly and at Passover), his mother's fears would be exceeded only by her trust in God.

REFLECTIONS FOR OUR OWN DISCIPLEHOOD

1. Each call is unique

We should not try to compare our whole lives with Mary's since our life's narrative is unique to us, just as Mary's is unique to her. The first words of the angel are without doubt the word of the Lord to all of us: children, women, and men: "Do not be afraid, you are blessed." The son of Mary has blessed each of us by living for us and dying and rising for us. We hear it as a promise substantiated; Mary heard it as a promise yet to be lived through. When we say to God in our prayers, "Here am I, your servant," we know more about our salvation than Mary did. Because of Mary's "Here am I" we can make ours with all the more assurance.

Mary was a female servant of God—the handmaid of the Lord: 50 percent or so of Christians are likely to be in that broad category. She was the mother of the Son of God. Since "to all who received him, who believed in his name, he gave power to become children of God" (John 1:12) all Christian mothers are mothers of children of God; all potential mothers are potential mothers of children of God. Mary was brought up serving God. may have the advantage of an early start over many, but it is whether we are servants of God today and tomorrow and at the end of our lives that will matter. It is unlikely that we will bypass death, but perhaps Mary's assumption is an example of the far-sighted wisdom of God. If Mary had been buried in a known tomb and her bones were still preserved, then, God forbid (as he has done), today someone might try to clone a son of Mary, inserting a Y chromosome into one of her cells to make a manmade Jesus!

2. Serving the Lord where we are

Our own vocations may never become truly clear, beyond an effort to serve God throughout the changes and chances of our earthly life. They may contain as many stumbling blocks as Jesus's life would seem to have without the eye of faith. Ours will contain episodes or instances of sin and obscured faith. If we think we have no sin we have at least the sins of spiritual blindness and pride. But we know the words to open ourselves again to God's grace, "Here am I, the servant of the Lord." We do not always have control over our lives, we are not always able to make decisions: for most of our lives we will be too young, too old, too bound by responsibility to children, to parents, to the frail or sick, to those to whom we have already contracted ourselves by marriage. In most people's lives there are relatively few pivotal moments when there are genuine decisions to be made about the course our life might take. We have little practice at making such decisions, and the reality of life is that many of us bungle our few genuine freedoms. Even Jesus's life *looks* mismanaged if you measure it in earthly success and failure, in popularity and enjoyment. The guiding hand of God often seems more visible in retrospect than in the present moment.

If we strive to serve God in every present moment and do everything as if we did it for him, then we are being his servants. Servants in a household do not make decisions to go on great quests for their master, but live where he appoints them, doing whatever small and repetitive or grand and responsible task he sets. The great thing is to be doing his work, or going about his business when he comes. Our own lives will have less significance on a cosmic scale than Mary's, but will be truly precious to God. If you doubt this, remember Jesus's words to the penitent thief, "*Today*, you will be *with me* in Paradise" (Luke 23:43). There was no standing in line behind the Son of God or the Patriarchs, but the promise was "today" and "with me."

Even when we know where our servanthood lies, we do not know the full course of it. Each day has enough anxieties of its own, and Jesus tells us not to waste our anxiety on tomorrow (Matthew 6:34). Every morning is a resurrection, a getting up again in spirit as well as body, every evening is a shedding of the day into God's mercy and keeping. What we regret is behind us, we cannot return to put it right or to wallow in its pain, but we can give it to God and accept his forgiveness. Every day is a new opportunity to serve God, to say, "Your kingdom come (today), your will be done (by me, today)." Each day we have a new chance to say with Mary, "Here am I, the servant of the Lord, let today unfold according to your will."

3. A vocation to marriage and parenthood

Mary was called out of the single state into motherhood and marriage. She models for us a person who has hearth and home to consider as well as her "walk with God." Her call announced for her the responsibility and commitment of motherhood. As soon as Joseph took her into his home (Matthew 1:24), she also had a spouse to consider and please.

Some Christian traditions have regarded marriage as a lesser vocation than the consecrated life, because the commitments of family render a person less available to God; one's time and energies are necessarily grounded in the daily needs of others. Yet Mary was called for her special service, out of the single life and into the family home. She gives inestimable status to the roles of wife and mother since the incarnation depended upon her accepting these roles. Joseph took the difficult role of the indispensable one who supports the enterprise, and he lived it with gracious dedication. Mary and her baby were utterly vulnerable and dependent on him during the nativity period, the flight into Egypt (Matthew 2:13), and the time spent as refugees in a foreign land. He protected and provided for them both.

Marriage is not an easy vocation even with God's hand directly upon it. Mary had a difficult start to her pregnancy. The miraculous element that set Jesus apart as Son of God made scope for public scandal and private mistrust. Mary's vocation needed the support of others, and this required Joseph in particular to be open to the message of the angel. Partnership in marriage is best served by partnership in faith. Where wife and husband have common ground in their prayer life and the degree of reality they accord to the service of God, then mutual support and understanding should follow. There should also be agreement about engendering real and living faith in any children of the union. The *Shema* urges us to impress the commandments on our children and, later in the chapter, verses 20–25 offer the retelling of the exodus story as the reason for serving God in the ways prescribed by the Commandments. The verses are worth reading to understand how Jews remember the exodus as if they took part in it and to be reminded that, *"the Lord commanded us to observe all these laws . . . so as to be happy forever and to live, as he has granted us to do until now"* (Deuteronomy 6:24). The Commandments describe "right living"—life lived in gratitude to God who heard the cry of the slaves and worked their liberation. The exodus is part of our Christian heritage, but the death and resurrection of Jesus takes precedence as the event that is made present for us by its remembrance, and is the chief showing of God's love that we respond to in prayer and deed.

Joseph disappears from the narrative after the famous visit to Jerusalem when Jesus was about twelve and stayed behind in the Temple "about his Father's business" (Luke 2:41–50). This was Jesus's coming of age. When a Jewish boy becomes *Bar Mitzvah*—son of the commandment—his father's responsibility for his religious life is over. The father says a prayer to thank God that the responsibility is accomplished. Jesus returned to Nazareth and lived under Mary and Joseph's authority, still a child in all other aspects of life. We do not know at what age Joseph died, but he does not figure as Mary does during the period of Jesus's ministry. When Jesus is dying he gives his mother into the care of John his closest disciple, and John takes her from the crucifixion site into his own home. Thus Mary continues to live out her life in a family community.

Mary embodies a number of homely virtues that come through the Gospel narrative. Throughout Jesus's infancy and childhood she cherishes and treasures the significant moments in her heart. Even when she doesn't understand her child, she allows him to be who he is and stores the memory so that she can reflect on the occasion later as its significance becomes clear. She raised an obedient child who found favor with people and with God. We all know it is not easy to please people and God simultaneously. It is easy to let God's standards slip in order to be more popular, and also easy to strive for God's standards in a manner that offends the people around us. Mary did a good job of raising her holy and well-integrated son. At Cana in Galilee she treads the tactful line between being the proud parent whose son can save the situation she has discreetly and sensitively noticed, and the parent who interferes in her adult son's career.

When a child has a vocation to the religious or missionary life, or simply to live his or her faith boldly and openly, it is natural to be fearful of the dangers, difficulties, or loneliness that might lie ahead. Mary teaches us to let our child walk God's path under God's care supported by our prayers and love. Whether or not we are parents, Mary teaches us to love her son, mingling our love with his so that we can feel compassion and concern for all his disciples and, with very great grace, for all those for whom he died.

4. Letting the Lord lead

Mark records Jesus's mother and family as concerned for his welfare. Joseph is not mentioned, and we presume he has died by this time. They think Jesus has gone mad and they do the concerned thing by coming to take him home (Mark 3:21). Two kinds of reports would have been reaching the family: on the one hand, Jesus's phenomenal success as a preacher and healer that now meant he was so beset by crowds he couldn't even have a meal; and on the other, dangerous, threatening murmurings against him by the Herodians, Pharisees, and scribes. The favored child had grown up, and his mission was on a collision course with the economic and political interests of the ruling parties. The Temple was the heart of Jewish identity. Roman tolerance of the religion was fragile, and the sacrifice industry was the money-spinner that paid the Roman soldiery to stay off the holy ground of the Temple Mount and to let the high priests live in villas fit for Roman gentlemen. The Romans maintained a show of control, for example by keeping the priestly robes in the Antonia Fortress that abutted and overlooked the Temple complex. The priests had to ask at the fortress for their robes, mindful of the grace of Rome that allowed them to practise monotheism instead of the pantheism of the rest of the empire. Any movement that aroused patriotic feeling, any potential claimant to the throne of David the warrior king, was dangerous to the uneasy truce. Jesus was stirring up a whirlwind of religious interest and could not help but become politically embroiled. The family has cause to be worried and comes in a body to rescue Jesus from himself.

Mark 3:31–35 and Luke 8:19–21 record Jesus's mother and brothers arriving, wanting to see him. In Matthew (12:46) they are anxious to have a word with him. We are not told whether he goes to them or makes them wait, but he makes a strange speech saying the crowd listening to him are his mother and brothers. We should understand this as elevating others to the affection in which Mary and his family were held rather than indifference to his blood relations. He is "at home" when he is among the people. Mary raised him in the spirit of the *Shema*, of constant mindfulness of what God requires. Jesus cannot moderate his popularity or his prophetic message to assist the scribes, Pharisees, priests, and Herodians who are in the difficult situation of their own efforts to balance personal position and Roman oversight. This is a point at which Mary has to accept that Jesus's heavenly Father is now the guiding principle in his life.

As you will have heard very often, no doubt, Mary models obedience to God. She models "Yes" without reservation, content to allow God to fill in the details of his seemingly impossible promise and to smooth the path with relatives who do not understand. Abraham and Sarah were promised a child (Genesis 15:4) to be conceived in the natural way. When the promise seemed slow in being fulfilled, and they doubted its performance since Abraham was in his seventies, they made their own arrangements for Abraham to conceive Ishmael with Sarah's slave girl Hagar. The long-promised Isaac was born to Sarah about fourteen years later, and Hagar and her child were sent away. Enmity between factions of Ishmael's and Isaac's descendants persists to this day. Mary's pregnancy followed immediately on the Annunciation, but she did not attempt to "take over," to steer the course of events herself. She allowed God to send her to Bethlehem when she was uncomfortably near her time, and to Egypt where no Jew would choose to go, as it was the "house of slavery" from which God had rescued their ancestors. Every Passover Mary and all other Jews would celebrate the Exodus as if they had taken part in it themselves—she would never choose to leave the Promised Land and go back there. Yet in God's wisdom it was the place of safety during the dangerous years of Herod the Great's jealousy.

We can often be tempted by our zeal for God to decide the course of our vocation for ourselves. We may, for example, feel called to ministry, we may sail through the selection procedure, our call affirmed at every stage including the sponsorship of the bishop and then "fail" the selection conference. Sometimes rejection will be beyond our human understanding and that of those who know us and are witness to our gifts and the service we have already performed with the grace of God. We may never recover from the pain of non-selection, but we must offer God the sacrifice of our pain and hand over to him once again the tiller of our desire to minister in his name. Anecdotal explanation for "failure" is similar to the driving test: "This year they're taking men with beards/evangelicals/women/people driving blue cars." The temptation is to lose faith in ourselves, God, or the Church. How else shall we explain the delusion of many years that God was lovingly, sometimes chidingly calling us to the ministry? Sometimes the sense of call persists loudly, stubbornly, and we just have to watch other candidates go forward where we long and feel called to be. Wherever a call feels thwarted or mistaken we must remember that the word of the Lord never returns to him empty. God who raises the dead will succeed with us in whatever he has chosen us for. We should ask him to keep calling us, keep us close to him, and make plain the work he has for us to do.

5. One great task

Mary was called to a single task—motherhood of the Son of God. It was a task that occupied the rest of her life. Even when Jesus was risen and ascended, her motherhood of him grew into the motherhood of the Church as symbolized by John taking her home from the crucifixion scene (John 19:27). Some people are called to a single important task that lasts for only a moment in their lives. In the Acts of the Apostles, Ananias—who is only described as a disciple, he holds no position in the church at Damascus—was called out of obscurity to lay hands on Saul, give him back his sight, and baptise him. He then returned to obscurity while Saul went on to define Christian teaching in the churches he set up and through his letters, which are still read in homes, schools, and churches today. Ananias and his friends might have thought one historically significant conversion role ought to pave the way for others, but one was all that the Lord asked of him. Ananias eventually saw the outcome of his work in Paul's successes; perhaps he reflected that the Lord had chosen in Paul the only man who could have achieved such a mission, and was glad to have been chosen for his part in Paul's conversion narrative. We may never know the outcome of work or works that the Lord has for us. A conversation with a stranger that turns to the things of God may redound for generations unbeknown to us; a seed sown in a friend may lie dormant or growing secretly for years until its blooming is so far removed in time that neither they nor we remember its sowing.

The sword of seeing her son rejected pierced Mary's soul as Simeon prophesied (Luke 2:35), yet she abandoned neither faith nor hope nor love nor yet obedience to her vocation of motherhood. She is an example to us of persistence in the most overwhelming distress and disappointment. She kept to her vocation while around her the disciples despaired and other men of God defied him through blindness or weakness. The news of his resurrection was a great affirmation of her faithfulness. There is no Gospel account of a specific meeting between the risen Jesus and his mother. She may of course have been with the disciples when he appeared to them through locked doors (John 20:19) and again when he appeared for Thomas (John 20:26), but it is reasonable to suggest that a meeting between Jesus and his mother, after all she had been through since the Annunciation, would be too private for us to trespass upon and that she treasured it secretly in her heart.

6. Called to transcend suffering

Mary models a life transformed by the presence of Jesus. She was called into suffering as an unmarried mother, a displaced person, a refugee, and through all the anxieties of a parent, magnified by the responsibility of mothering the Son of God. She was also called to transcend suffering: to allow it to be God's will and purpose leading to a glorious and unexpected conclusion. She teaches us to bear adversity and uncertainty patiently, trusting in God. Answering God's call always leads to a change in orientation, sometimes a complete change in career or lifestyle. Sometimes it leads us through suffering to the place where God would have us be. The joy of childbirth follows the pain of labor; and the joy of resurrection follows the misery of dying. In the process of responding to God's call our own plans may have to die; some former habits or negative personality traits may need to be let go. The balance of pain and joy will depend on whether we focus our gaze on the dying or the resurrection. Crucifixion is not firstly about suffering: it is firstly about doing God's will. Understanding this moves us on from "let this cup pass me by" to "thy will be done" (Mark 14:32–34). Mary teaches us to be God's vessels, humbly allowing God to fill us and direct us for his purposes, whether the great work belongs to us or to those whom we support in our domestic or the wider church family.

7. The holy family and entertaining angels

Mary's narrative teaches us to be careful how we treat people who are in unconventional situations or circumstances and for whom we have no natural sympathy. We accept the Annunciation without condemnation of the single mother. We may shake our heads at Joseph's lack of faith in Mary and God but we have the benefit of knowing the end of the story, the resurrection that justifies everything that went before. Jesus's neighbors, who did not have the same benefit, felt favorably toward the young man as he grew up but turned against him when he began preaching and specifically when he said that Isaiah's prophecy, "The spirit of the Lord is upon me," had come true in their hearing. They tried to throw him off a cliff (Luke 4:14–30) and he could barely work any miracles in his home community (Mark 6:1–6). This is a grave lesson against the "Who does he think he is?" attitude.

We would not like to be Pilate and find out we had crucified the Son of God against our better judgement. We would not like to hear that the man we crucified had risen and was appearing to people through locked doors—we might be scared indeed! I am not proposing that every illegitimate child is the Son of God and every criminal is an innocent person bearing the guilt of others. Jesus did not scorn to share these unfavorable situations when he came to live among his people. By sharing them he blessed them and sanctified them as places where God may be found and out of which God's work may be done.

Jesus said, "Where I am there will my servant be" (John 12:26). We should not scorn to be among any whom God is calling into companionship and blessing. We should make our churches open to all people regardless of social status and social desirability. The Old Testament tells us once that we should love our neighbor (Leviticus 19:18) and thirty times that we should love the stranger. It is natural and easy to love those who are like us. It is less natural and may be hard to love those who are not like us, so we need to be told thirty times more frequently that loving God means loving the stranger. Jesus's parable of the good Samaritan tells us our neighbor and the stranger are the same person.

The Nazarenes did not recognize Jesus as the Holy One of God and responded to him badly; the Letter to the Hebrews tells us others have done better and have entertained angels unawares (Hebrews 13:2). If angels came in shining clothes with wings we would be afraid, but nevertheless welcome them and give them the best. Angels, possibly God and his angels, possibly the Holy Trinity, visited Abraham as strangers in the desert (Genesis 18:1–15) and he entertained them and received a repetition of the founding promise of the Judaeo-Christian tradition, "Sarah shall have a son." In Matthew 25:31–46 Jesus teaches us that what we do for the least of our brethren we do for him. Let us not be caught out saying, "Lord, when was I unwelcoming or unfriendly to you?" or "When did I not want to sit next to you in church?", etc.

8. An uncomfortable faith

Faith is often described as a comfort. It is both a comfort and a shake-up. The events that Mary's faith brought her to were not very comfortable, yet she has the most wonderful, intimate relationship with God. The closer in we get, the more we find faith is not superficial. It is not an activity; it is life, and all around us are people with God-shaped holes in their lives to whom we may be called, like Mary, to carry Christ. This is not aggressive evangelism but bringing his qualities to bear on our dealings so that we carry ourselves with his grace. We bring him near to those who do not know him so that they can see he is the "completion" of our lives. We serve him best when we let him take control, when we are able to say, "I am the servant of the Lord."

Questions for reflection or group discussion

(Question 1 can be discussed in general terms: domestic confidentiality need not be shared.)

1. (a) Do you think of your place in family life as a vocation?
   (b) What difference might this make to (i) your satisfaction with your "lot" and (ii) the effort you put into your relationships?
2. (a) What kind of oversight/mentoring/companionship do you exercise in your children's relationship with God?
   (b) Is your children's relationship with their heavenly Father as much your concern as their relationship with their earthly father? (Do mothers and fathers give different answers to this question?)
3. (a) Mary (and Joseph) had a difficult beginning to her pregnancy. She was widowed young and her first-born son was condemned as a criminal. How does your church reach out to families in unconventional situations or trauma?
   (b) Jesus spent time with the disreputable. He could not be "contaminated" by them but reintegrated them into society through his influence not his condemnation. Is your church a place where social stigma can be healed and forgotten? Can you make it so?

Additional Bible readings

- Compare the song of Hannah with the song of Mary (the Magnificat)—1 Samuel 2:1–10 and Luke 1:46–55. Hannah's song seems to have a more triumphant, exultant ring to it, while Mary sings the same themes in a quieter, humbler tone.

Remember that Hannah suffered for her barrenness, which the Lord has now taken away. Mary's conception was unsought and even more awesome than the miraculous conceptions of Hannah and Elizabeth.

Summary of key themes
- Mary let the Lord lead her life. It took her where she would not have chosen to go and gave her great pain, yet also unimaginable joys. The Lord has a similar quality of joy in store for us.
- Obedience to God liberates us into intimate relationship with him.
- Nothing we do in obedience to God is "lost" or ultimately futile.
- We are called to "carry Christ" with us as we go about our daily business and not leave him in our prayer corner or our church.

Take-home message to think and pray about
- God is our Father and our children's Father. How do we make this more than just a prayer?

Prayer projects
- Pray for God-with-us to be manifest amid situations Jesus sanctified by being there in the circumstances of his own life: domestic difficulty, single parenthood, living far from home, trial, and punishment.
- Pray for the parents and infants in your local toddler group and maternity department—that they may glimpse the wonder of Jesus born as a human child.

Prayer

Here am I, the servant of the Lord.
Make me humble to do the simple tasks with joy;
give me courage when I am afraid of what you are asking;
comfort me when I think you ask too much;
affirm me with your real presence, Lord;
console me with deep knowledge of your love.
Let it be with me according to your word.
Amen.

3

HERE AM I, SEND ME: ISAIAH

*This chapter considers the call of Isaiah.
We can read about his vision of God and his
reply in Isaiah 6.*

BACKGROUND

Isaiah received his call in 740 BCE, the year that King Uzziah died. He was closely connected with the royal court at Jerusalem in the kingdom of Judah and had significant influence there. Rabbinic tradition says he was nephew to King Amaziah. His career as a prophet lasted some forty years with his last dateable prophecies referring to Sennacherib's invasion in 701. According to Jewish tradition he was sawn in two during a persecution of the faithful by King Manasseh. The writer to the Hebrews may be referring to Isaiah in Hebrews 11:37.

Isaiah had a formal ministry as a prophet, acting as the mouthpiece of God, saying, "Thus says the Lord." His mission was to announce the fall of the two kingdoms of Israel and Judah as the punishment for unfaithfulness on a national scale. Under Kings Uzziah and then Jotham, Judah and Israel were at peace with each other and their neighbors. They were bordered by vassal states and were developing the countries' resources and their trade. Judah was outwardly prosperous and secure but inwardly suffering from corruption and social and religious decay. This was a state of affairs of which Isaiah was painfully aware (Isaiah 6:5) and he knew that the Holy One of Israel—his characteristic name for God—would not let it go unpunished. A thoroughgoing judgment was approaching that would leave only a small, faithful remnant. The remnant would look as unpromising as the stump of a tree cut down, but through it God would vindicate himself.

Beyond the terrifying judgement of invasions, Isaiah saw a future time when the remnant of Israel (speaking as if the kingdoms were united) would rebuild peace and justice under a son (descendant) of David. The remnant features in the verses following his call and forms a persistent and characteristic part of his teaching. Isaiah makes short-term political prophecies that are rapidly fulfilled. He foresaw a Messianic king described at 9:6 in a verse we use at Christmas, "Unto us a child is born, unto us a son is given . . . He shall be called Wonderful Counselor, Mighty God, Everlasting Father, Prince of Peace." This king is like the new branch shooting from the tree stump. In Isaiah 11:2–3 the prophet sees the fulsome Spirit of God resting on him and a beatific reign ensues. Isaiah expected this king to defeat the Assyrians within his lifetime. Christians associate the king with Jesus. Isaiah saw both present and future through God's eyes and tried to call the people back to a sense of duty, obedience, and love toward God.

ISAIAH'S CALL

Isaiah's call sets a pattern for so many people's own experience of God. We recognize the process of encountering God for certain, being reactively aware of sin, healed of it, and made fit for service. Isaiah sees God the King in all his overwhelming majesty and glory. He himself is present in the normally hidden court as if by special invitation. The narrative marks the transition from having heard of God, to being on personal terms with him (see Job 42:5). Isaiah sees God for real and does not expect to survive the experience, hence the cry of woe at his consuming awareness of his own sin and the sin that surrounds him. Sin prevents Isaiah from rejoicing in God's presence like the angels, so the angel brings a burning coal from the altar, touches his lips, and pronounces him clean. Only after he is cleansed of sin at heaven's initiative (and not by his own efforts) does Isaiah hear the invitation to serve: "Whom shall I send, and who will go for us?" And Isaiah replies, "Here am I, send me!"

The call is a model for all (first) encounters with God: awareness of God's glory; contrasting, devastating awareness of personal sin; cleansing; and then readiness to serve. The cleansing is important because, as Jesus taught, a person cannot serve two masters (Matthew 6:24); he will love (put first) one, and hate (give lower priority to) the other. Those who use the sacrament of reconciliation will know how light and clean and single-minded a person feels after absolution. A person can only set out to serve God wholeheartedly when free of the doubts and compromises of sin.

REFLECTIONS FOR OUR OWN DISCIPLEHOOD

1. Forgiven means fit for service

Every forgiven sinner is fit for the service of God. There are no forgiven sins that hinder God from asking in your hearing, "Whom shall I send and who will go for us?" and there are no forgiven sins that hinder you from answering, "Here am I, send me."

It is the person who is most acutely aware of his or her sin in the light of God's purity who will be most sensitive to the miracle of being made clean, and feel most urgently compelled to share the good news. For the Christian this awareness arises through Isaiah-like contemplation of God's majesty in the court of heaven, and also through contemplation of Jesus's passion and crucifixion and thence the weight of *our* sin, which is forgiven at such cost to him. Isaiah was not a notorious sinner, yet he felt the weight of his own and his community's sinfulness. His own sins were doubtless small in comparison to those of certain people he could name if he had a mind to do so, but, in the presence of God, judging his neighbors was not his business or concern. Bright light shows our shadows, which hide when the light is dim. When Isaiah was confronted with the sight of God, his sins were a real concern. Education and tradition taught the Pharisee of Jesus's parable (Luke 18:9–14) that the personal God of Abraham, Isaac, and Jacob was present in the Temple. He knew that when Solomon dedicated the original temple built on that spot, the *shekinah* or glory of God moved in. He knew this with his mind, but not with his spirit. If he had been spiritually aware of God's presence he would never have compared himself with the tax collector. In spite of all his care to keep the Commandments, fast twice a week and pay tithes on all his wealth, he would have said with Isaiah, "Woe is me for I am a man of unclean lips and . . . my eyes have seen the King." And he would have meant it. His lack of spiritual awareness rendered him unloving and unforgiven.

In Luke 7:47, Jesus said to Simon the Pharisee: "Whoever has been forgiven little, shows only a little love." Conversely, this would mean that those who have been forgiven much show a great deal of love. We might misunderstand this to suggest that a cradle Christian's love for God and neighbor is automatically inferior to that of a reformed, notorious sinner. I believe that the "little" or "much" of our forgiveness is linked to how "little" or "much" we are aware of our sin in contrast to God's purity, and that our love is in similar proportion.

People who received miracles from Jesus wanted to follow him and witness to him wherever he went. Two examples are Bartimaeus cured of blindness (Luke 18:35–43), who followed Jesus glorifying God so that the people praised God too, and the Geresene demoniac (Mark 5:1–20), who was not allowed to follow Jesus but was sent by him to tell his own amazed countrymen what God had done for him. Such people had a tale to tell with enthusiasm and wonder, and they played their part in spreading the gospel. Disciples who were closer to Jesus—Peter, Andrew, James, John, Levi (Matthew)—followed him at the simple command, "Follow me." They were drawn to him by the unarticulated recognition of God-with-us. When Simon Peter was finally able to put his finger on it after Jesus had been teaching the crowd and then provided a miraculous catch of fish (Luke 5:8–11) it came out as, "Go away from me, Lord, for I am a sinful man." Simon had already been called into special friendship with Jesus: Jesus had been to his house; he had cured Simon's mother-in-law; Simon had seen others healed and heard demons calling Jesus the Son of God. He was comfortable being close to Jesus until the penny dropped who Jesus was, and then his sins rose up and accused him and he was appalled at being a sinner in the presence of the Lord. Jesus gave the characteristic response, "Do not be afraid," and then told him his commission, "from now on you will be catching people."

Simon the Pharisee (Luke 7:36–50) had no real awareness of love in his relationship with God: it was almost a business contract in which he played his part by keeping the rules conscientiously and accurately. He had a certain pride in his success and enjoyed the status of Pharisee, which means "pure one." His vision of goodness was limited to the rules that he kept and that the woman who had entered his house uninvited failed to keep. The woman's vision of goodness stretched all the way to Jesus, from whom emanated the love that said, "Come to me, all who are burdened with life and sin and I will take your burden from you" (compare this with Matthew 11:28).

In Jesus the woman saw one who truly was pure and whose purity was like a white hole drawing her out of the shadows into purifying light. Jesus brought the miracle of wanting her to draw near *because she was a sinner*, not wanting to repel her for that same reason. He wanted her to come close and be washed and re-formed in his goodness. Simon's vision of purity was so lacking that he thought Jesus would be contaminated by the woman and she should not be allowed near him. The woman with the haemorrhages was in a similar predicament (Mark 5:25–34). She was ritually impure and anyone who touched her would become ritually impure too. She was afraid to present herself to Jesus lest she contaminate the holy teacher. She touched the fringes of his garment secretly—the symbol of the laws that condemned her to isolation and loneliness and kept her out of the Temple—and the power flowed from him to her. Purity overcame impurity and she was healed. We believe that the light shines in the darkness and the darkness has never overcome it (John 1:5). That is one of the most powerful symbols of our hope. A single candle flame is apparently visible for two miles in complete darkness.

The church is a community of people called to be saints. We must all allow all of our fellow pilgrims to make the transition from sinner to saint. That transition is "getting up" to new life, like Lazarus's resurrection. Resurrection is getting up again, whether from sin, sickness, or death. Jesus said "Unbind him, let him go" (John 11:44). He says the same to our past and to all who remember it. The same truth persists, however many times we need to get up and try again.

2. Knowing we are forgiven

The seraph said to Isaiah, "Now that this has touched your lips, your guilt has departed and your sin is blotted out." These are splendid words. Your guilt *has* departed—the action is completed, blame and guilt are well and truly gone; and your sin is blotted out—it remains so in the continuing present. The seraph says sin, not sins, to convey a total cleansing of thought, word, deed, and inclination, so that there is no trace of impurity remaining. One action of burning away the dross is effective forever. This was well and good for Isaiah, who experienced the vision with the full force of a reality that exceeds the reality of the material world, but what about those who have not experienced such conviction?

Firstly we can take Isaiah's vision on trust as if he experienced and recorded it for the benefit of all who come after him. We can let his certainty count for us. Secondly Catholics and Anglicans have access to the sacrament of reconciliation. For Catholics this is prescribed at least once a year; for Anglicans the ruling is, "all may, some should, none must."

Since the sacrament of reconciliation (formerly the sacrament of confession) is so easily misunderstood, it is worth explaining in some detail. (In what follows the priest is referred to as "he," but in the Anglican Church the priest could also be "she." With regard to the penitent, "he" should be deemed to include "she.") In the Garden of Eden, Adam and Eve gave in to the persuasion of the serpent and did something expressly forbidden by God. Their joy of living deteriorated from that point. Eating the apple brought them a sense of shame at being naked. This is like a physical expression of the spiritual shame of disobedience, a reflected pain. Because they felt exposed—physically and spiritually—they hid from God instead of enjoying his company. They said they were hiding because they were naked, speaking of the physical symptom of their fear of coming before him, not the spiritual cause. The Lord knew what they had done and they made excuses for it, seeking to avoid blame. Their easy life in Eden was at an end and so was their innocent relationship with God. The murder of their younger son by his jealous brother is only a chapter away. Genesis chapter 3 is an allegory of everyone's life. If there is no way back, we remain at a distance from God, afraid to be too closely in his presence. Jesus is called the new Adam (see 1 Corinthians 15:45), the new start for all humankind. His obedience and his death and resurrection undo the alienation that follows our disobedience. We are reconciled with God through him, hence the sacrament of reconciliation.

Sacramental confession exists to keep people close to God. No one should fall away from God out of despair over his or her sins. Some people feel "God could never forgive me," but the priest will assure them with the authority Jesus gave to his disciples (Matthew 16:19) that "the Lord *has put away* your sin." There is no doubt and no despair. It is to remedy despair that the Anglican Church suggests, "some should" use the sacrament of reconciliation. The paralysed man in Mark 2:1–12 would never have got on with his life if Jesus had not told him, with authority, face to face, that his sins were forgiven.

A sacrament is an outward and visible sign of an inward and spiritual grace. The Church does something we can see so that we know God is doing something we cannot see. Reconciliation is something we can definitely feel. People report a sense of lightness, cleanness, well-being, overflowing love for all people, overwhelming love of God, closeness to God, sudden understanding of the power of and overwhelming gratitude for Jesus's death and resurrection, renewed determination to stay close to Jesus, etc. Those who use the sacrament know it to be powerful and good, and an experience akin to that described by Isaiah. They become more outward looking and more ready to serve.

This is how it works. The penitent person makes a prayerful examination of his or her conscience, identifying the things that are incompatible with the love of God and that form the kind of barrier Isaiah articulated by saying, "Woe is me! I am lost for I am a man of unclean lips [and thoughts and actions] yet my eyes have seen the King, the Lord of hosts." Some books contain lists of sins or lists of ways of breaking the (spirit of the) Ten Commandments, but I suggest that when a person seriously contemplates the majesty of God or the pain of the crucifixion those things that need forgiveness will raise themselves in accusation all by themselves.

The penitent then presents himself to the priest by appointment and receives a blessing. He tells God in the presence of the priest those things he has thought, said, and done that offend against the love of God. This does not have to be desperately specific because God knows the detail and it is to him that the confession is made. The point is to be genuinely sorry, as the woman was at the house of Simon the Pharisee, and, as in her case, tears often accompany heartfelt sorrow. The woman's confession was wordless, but sacramental reconciliation does require the penitent to speak their confession. The person sums up their confession by saying, "For these and all my sins which I cannot now remember I am truly sorry." This catch-all is not to cover up sins one is ashamed to name but to avoid the person rushing back five minutes later when they remember something else and fear they have not made an adequate confession or have not been forgiven the last thing.

The most obstructive sin to reconciliation is pride. No one should omit sins because they are ashamed for the priest to hear what they have done. If a person will not name the sin out of shame, it still has control over them and will not be removed from their conscience by the rite of reconciliation. Naming a sin gives you ownership and control over it: it helps you regain the ground for Christ. What is sin that it should have power over anyone and compel them to keep it as a dark secret? Jesus has already defeated sin; it is a lie that you cannot own up and claim the forgiveness he has already won for you. We teach our children that hiding the pieces is worse than breaking the vase. The same is true with our lives.

The point of confession is that one confesses to God things he knows you have done. What God is seeking is our awareness, admission, sorrow, and desire for him to take our guilt away and blot out our sin. To do this he requires us to tell him everything we want him to take away. Jesus says, "Ask and you shall receive." To underline the fact that we are confessing to God, the priest in whose presence we confess need not even speak our language! The best arrangement is to have a spiritual director whom we can see regularly and with whom the sacrament of reconciliation is only part of our progress report on our spiritual journey.

Whoever the priest is, he has no continuing interest in our list of sins, he will not remember it and he will not discuss it with anyone else. If we have reason not to trust a local priest, or he is not *au fait* with the sacrament, we can make an appointment with someone else. Among priests who "hear" confession, confessing to a stranger is a well-understood practice. In some parishes the priest has a reciprocal arrangement with a colleague so that parishioners can receive the sacrament of reconciliation from someone other than himself.

At the end of the confession part the penitent asks the priest for advice, penance, and absolution. Sins are a symptom of how we respond to life and so the advice will suggest how to avoid repeating the particular sins the person is sorry to have committed. The advice comes from the priestly store of grace, wisdom, experience, and listening to God. Penance is usually a suitable prayer, but it can be some act of service. It will include accepting the cross we have to bear in life (rather than resenting it, which would be a sin). If the penance is a prayer the person will pray it when leaving the priest after the absolution and take some quiet time with God to thank him for the life-giving gift of forgiveness. The person may also find it helpful to pray it in the ensuing days as an armor against falling back into sin. If the penance is an act of service, the person will begin it as soon as is practically possible. Zacchaeus chose his own penance in his form of confession to Jesus: "If I have cheated anyone, I will repay them fourfold." In sacramental reconciliation the priest gives the penance because people are liable to inflict unnecessarily harsh penalties on themselves. Jesus has paid the price of our sin. We do not need to try to pay it as well. The aim of the penance is to help us come closer to Jesus who has taken away our sin.

The absolution can take different forms, for example: "By the authority given to me, I absolve you from all your sins in the name of the Father, the Son, and the Holy Spirit" or "The Lord has put away your sin" or some other words. Finally the priest asks us to pray for him because he is a sinner too. Even if the first form of words is used, we must understand that the priest is only articulating, for the penitent to hear and believe, something that the Lord has already done. When Jesus forgave the woman at Simon the Pharisee's house, he was confirming something that had already taken place. The narrative tells us that her sins *have been forgiven* (Luke 7:47). Her love is her "thank you" for God's forgiveness. In verses 49 and 50 Jesus confirms this truth out loud in an authoritative way for the woman and the guests to know so that she and her critics can leave the sin in the past where it belongs and where it no longer condemns her. Sacramental reconciliation gives the penitent, privately, the same authoritative assurance that the sins confessed no longer stand between the person and their Lord.

Sin is like a shield deflecting God: when it is "put away" God can come in and make his home with us. Reconciliation (whether sacramental or private) involves risk and vulnerability because we open ourselves fully to his intimate presence and grace. The meeting with God is not between equals: it is between Creator and created; Redeemer and redeemed; Savior and saved. We are familiar with the nervousness engendered when the headmaster wants to speak to us, or a police officer is driving behind us. We can imagine being nervous if we were to meet the Queen. However much we love and are loved by God we are not equals, and the awareness of his greatness can be disturbing. Isaiah was overwhelmed by the disparity *"Woe is me . . . my eyes have seen the King."* Although the presence of God is awesome, the message is always "Do not be afraid," because God's love draws us through the appalling recognition of our sin into a sharing of his purity at his instigation and cost. The experience of God is transforming. *Knowing* what we have hitherto *believed* changes our priorities. There is nothing provisional about our relationship with God: it comes first and last and embraces everything in between.

Being cleansed of sin is liberating. As the Book of Common Prayer says, "If we say we have no sin we deceive ourselves and the truth is not in us." It is an evasion that Jesus disapproved of to say we are not as bad as others (see the Pharisee and the tax collector in Luke 18:10–14). Even self-criticism is difficult to take in this modern age, but for the Christian it is the only way through the glass ceiling to a clearer knowledge of God. Sometimes the order of

Isaiah's experience is reversed so that it is through self-examination, sorrow, and repentance that we come into awareness of the Lord waiting and wanting us to enjoy his presence unencumbered by a heavy conscience.

Sacramental confession is not a way of life for all Christians. Yet it is right and proper and automatic to bewail our sin when we are aware of God; hence acts of worship have a congregational confession very near the start so that whatever keeps us at a distance from him and obstructs his word from finding its home in us is dealt with. We must believe fully that God blots out our sins completely so that he does not remember them. When they are forgiven they are gone from us—"as far as the East is from the West, so far has he set our sins from us" (Psalm 103:12). They no longer weigh us down or stand between us and the worship and service of God. If God discloses himself to us, he has already chosen us. Jesus said, "no one can come to me unless it is granted by the Father" (John 6:65). This step, from believing to knowing for certain and being on personal terms with the Lord, is given by God. God says to the whole court of heaven, "Whom shall I send and who will go for us?" Anyone who is listening can answer the invitation, saying, "Here am I, send me."

3. What am I called to do?

When we are conscious of being in the presence of God and "hear" God asking us who will go for him, the particular mission may be different from when Isaiah or our neighbor gave an answer. It will be the mission God is hoping we will volunteer for. It may be to the priesthood or religious or missionary life, in which case the Church will go through a discernment process to agree that call with us, or to suggest God is calling us to a different way of life. For the greater number of people it may be to live the convinced and manifestly loving way of discipleship where we are, in our family, at school, at work, in our locality. Just as the magi returned from honoring the Christchild by another way (Matthew 2:12), so we may find that our invitation is "Who will go for us along this better way of discipleship?" "Who will go bravely carrying their certainty in a world that rejects and despises the way of love?"

4. Here are we, send us

The Church has always been a *community* of service. The Acts of the Apostles tells us the earliest examples of church work (see Acts 4:33–34, 6:1). You may feel called to pray about ways the Lord might be asking a group of you to "go for him" among certain of his people. Perhaps there are some in need of human contact. Perhaps you can serve tea and coffee or soup and a roll in church to let people get out of the house and give them some company and conversation. In rural areas this might be something good to offer on the day the bus doesn't run, or when it gets back on market day. Once you have contact with people other things can flow—a toddler service, discussion or prayer groups, help for homebound people who have no one to change a lightbulb for them. You may discover reasons people don't come to Sunday church—pregnant people, mothers with young children, and the elderly are put off if there is no toilet. Can you install one?

If your church is near an elementary school, perhaps you can offer cups of tea or coffee and quiet time to busy moms when they drop their children off in the morning. If you are near a middle school, high school or college, can you offer coffee and sanctuary during the weeks of finals and midterms? Do you have a parish room that could be used for quiet study by those who find it difficult to study at home, even for an hour a day? If you are near a daycare or nursing home can you offer worship that suits the children or the residents' needs? You might start with a carol service or anniversary thanksgiving. Like any other enterprise, these efforts will require prayerful consideration, market research, and marketing – ideally on a person-to-person basis.

Unlike other organizations the Church exists for those who are not members and is often making itself available to those who don't yet know their need. Take-up of the services you believe God is calling you to offer may be slow, but the knowledge that something is available is often a great comfort. Above all, making contact and raising the profile normalizes the Christian worldview and normalizes the reference to God throughout the business of living. When church activities are part of the community's vocabulary it becomes obvious to ask for God's blessing and assistance (and to say thank you afterward). It is not an embarrassment in the crises of life, including sickness and death, to offer prayers or the preparation of the dying. The church is a normal place to visit for a little sit, a little prayer, or a little quiet. It can be a stepping aside from the stress of life, a proper oasis of God's peace and of his promise that all shall be well.

5. Can you see the King?

Try to have your church open for prayer. The church is where people have a promise that God hears them. If security is a problem have a few well-publicized hours on days that seem to be best—two hours on a Sunday and Tuesday afternoon or a time when some good souls can sit in the church and read the Bible or a spiritual book or spend time in prayer and listening to God. It may be a rare occasion when someone visits, but you never truly know how good it was that they were able to come in.

Try to have your church looking and feeling like a place where people pray. If your maintenance staff and fire department allow it, candles are a brilliant way to create a community of prayer. Lighting a candle gives us "something to do"—a physical token of the prayers said. The flame is the promise of light in darkness, God's presence that the darkness cannot overcome. It goes on burning as if the prayer remains in God's presence when the prayerful depart. When other visitors enter, they can tell that someone has prayed here. The place is established as a communication point. There is a sense of praying together while separated in time, a sense that one is not alone in having come here to be with God. To someone entering in distress a candle is another person's trust in the light and life of God. This is trust upon which a distressed person can rely when his or her own hope or confidence is small. "Lord, I believe, help thou my unbelief" (Mark 9:24).

Small signs of the activity of prayer can be immeasurably supportive. I know of a church where people write their prayer requests in a book; when the vicar has prayed for the intention he initials and dates the book. If the person returns they can see that he has added his prayers to theirs. Jesus liked to gather a supportive community of prayer—see the raising of the little girl (Mark 5:21–42)—and he said,

"Where two or three are gathered in my name, I am there among them" (Matthew 18:20). As discussed in the chapter on Samuel, two or three witnesses prove a point, in this case that Jesus is present.

6. God's man at work

We reflected on Samuel's single state and Mary being called into marriage. Isaiah was probably married. There is no real concept of the single state in Judaism since all Jews are under the commandment delivered to humanity at creation and repeated to Noah after the flood, "Be fruitful, multiply" (Genesis 1:28; 9:1). He certainly had a son with a prophetess (Isaiah 8:3) and the name he gave his son (Speed-spoil-hasten-plunder!) was part of his prophetic message. Isaiah was called to fatherhood as part of his ministry, yet we know little of his family circumstances. We will look instead at Isaiah as the model of "God's man (person) in the workplace."

Isaiah had a high-powered, high-pressure job. He was well connected and moved in powerful, probably ruthless, circles. Royal courts have famously been places of risk, intrigue, valued "yes" men, elaborate lip service, and complicated power games. Survival is more surely guaranteed by a strong instinct for self-preservation than by a consuming zeal for integrity. This may sound like a caricature of somebody's office, boardroom, or staffroom. The politics of human interaction and advancement are universal throughout time. Isaiah was called to be a whistle blower, to deliver an unpopular message—in vivid and explicit terms—about consequences coming home to roost.

If Isaiah is our model in the workplace, he is a model of integrity. He has absolute faith in God, whom he has seen, and knows that he is accountable to him. His sense of woe on encountering the holiness of God helps him look out at life with God's perspective. Our role as a Christian in the workplace may be as a voice of conscience, a human voice thinking with our heart as well as our head. We can stand out as a person of integrity who sees the whole picture, who understands the human impact of company policy and practice. If we are a "footsoldier" in our organization we can still exert an example of integrity, from punctuality and good timekeeping to customer service and good relationships with our colleagues and seniors. Integrity is contagious even if it works through the back door of putting others to shame rather than the front door of inspiring emulation.

7. Reaching out to the lapsed

Isaiah delivered his message to the lapsed. The memory of God was close to the surface, many were still going through the motions of worship but for want of humility before God and observance of his teaching, the Hebrew world was falling into anarchy and was absolutely vulnerable to division and invasion. Israel was built on the mighty intervention of God to rescue Israel from slavery, yet the temptation was always at hand for the king to manage things himself so that he could steer events to the best outcome he could foresee. Isaiah counseled faith in God rather than alliances with other nations and foresaw a time of restoration and future peace and justice under one of King David's descendants. His prophecies oscillate between the terrifying "day of the Lord" that sweeps in with invading armies committing atrocities, and the joy of relationship with God restored and fortunes renewed. With the establishment of the monarchy the prophet was no longer the mouthpiece of God, but a kind of go-between reminding the king that it was God's people he governed.

Old Testament prophecies are full of the call to "return to the Lord." Encouraging the lapsed back into active faith is a task accessible to many of us. These are our family, friends, neighbors, and former members of our congregations, who have fallen away out of loss of habit, lack of encouragement, lack of progress in faith, disappointment in life, a disagreement with the vicar or priest or a leading light in the church community, a perceived snub, etc. Often the reasons are neither here nor there, but practice makes permanent and once the churchgoing habit is lost, to regain it is like climbing a mountain.

These people who are already known to us ought to be a more receptive (and less scary) mission field than the completely unchurched. They have an inkling or a memory, or have heard the rumor of the reality of God. Often deep down they envy your certainty but are lodged in an inertia that contains some resistance to the effort and commitment required by a return. Perhaps there is a little guilt at falling away; perhaps a scoffing family member whom it is easier to appease than defy. The "church occasion" is a marvelous opportunity for these people to step back through the door and find themselves at home once more. It is easy to justify going to church for a "special," particularly if so-and-so has invited them and will drive them and there are refreshments afterward and it all sounds very harmless to the people at home who worry about enthusiasm in religion. A church can put on numerous "specials" in a year until, without realizing it, the lost sheep has come home and it is no big deal to fill in the gaps between the occasions—in fact, to miss an ordinary Sunday would feel like "missing out."

A church can begin with the folk festivals to encourage back the deeply lapsed. These are Christmas, Easter, Mother's Day, Thanksgiving, All Saints Day. Barely anyone can object to going on these occasions, and each can be made into a very special service reaching the loving touch of God into ordinary lives. More "churchy" specials can be arranged on festivals with dramatic (enacted) liturgies or that lend themselves to a good social afterwards. If a neighboring parish can join you for a service and a party it makes for a bigger community of prayer and helps to "normalize" the whole business for those who feel conspicuous in a church. Some examples would be: Shrove Tuesday with pancake fun and games afterward; Ash Wednesday with its liturgy of ashing adding new sight and touch to the experience; the Easter Triduum of Maundy Thursday, Good Friday, and Holy Saturday with the respective dramatic liturgies; a celebration of the anniversary of the church's founding, which can be turned into a lively party—invite the bishop to preach and your neighboring parishes to celebrate at your Communion service and party.

Country parishes might introduce a celebration of the beginning of the agricultural season with a "plough Sunday"—get a plough as near as you can to the church and bless it and all the work of your parishioners; get out among the growing crops during the growing season and ask God's blessing on our food and the daily progress of life; cut the first sheaf of corn in the nearest field and process with it to church on Thanksgiving. The out-of-doors element is fun, invites the curious to attend, and provides opportunities for witness and conversation. It shows that God is not locked in the church from Sunday to Sunday but sought and found in the realms of daily toil and food. He is God of bread and wine: of everyday and of celebration.

The key ingredient to any special service is an authentic holiness so that those who have found an excuse to come have the opportunity to be touched by God and hear the call of his real presence. Never think a "special" should be a lighter diet than usual, or some form of entertainment. If you are not in earnest about worshiping the Lord of Hosts with due respect and reverence, how will your visitors know that he is real and not just an idea in the mind of the church? A "special" ought to be more than usually moving. It is feeling the presence of God that will bring the people back on Sunday.

Make a huge deal of baptisms and confirmations as milestones in a person's relationship with God— no church has so many young people that they don't need to be particularly welcomed and special. Send the baptized children an anniversary card for the next five years, invite the family to church on the nearest Sunday to the baptism anniversary and pray for them. Consolidate your young confirmed into a group that has fun and continues learning about faith and makes a real contribution to the worship and service of the church community. You might join several parishes together to make a group so the young don't feel isolated and you ensure they have the option of "Christian activities" as well as secular ones. Their faith needs to make a difference in their lives, and the church should try to help them be different and do different things (safe from ridicule) because they are Christian. The church may be the first forum in which they are regarded as adult participants. Declaration of belief made *with their own mouths and from their own hearts* is indeed a proof of maturity and it signifies ownership of that personal relationship modeled by Samuel, Mary, and Isaiah that leads into service of God and his people.

8. Awaiting God's moment

In spite of the message that accompanies his call in the Bible narrative, Isaiah does not seem to have exercised his ministry straight away but to have had four years of consolidation during the reign of Jotham. He bides God's time to warn of the coming judgment. The judgment is both a cleansing and pruning of the nation. To a vine dresser both words mean cutting back to encourage fruitfulness. Jesus uses this sort of language in his teaching on the true vine at John 15. The vineyard is a frequent allegory for Israel. The judgment is also a reducing of the population, showing that the strength of the nation cannot possibly be in its people but in God. This is like the drastic reduction of forces in Gideon's army to show that it is God who wins the battle (Judges 7:2–7).

Your first conviction of God is probably not the starting signal for evangelism in a hostile world. You will probably share your story first within the sympathetic and glad community of believers. Jesus had a magnificent experience of God in his baptism yet withdrew into the wilderness to pray and consolidate before starting his teaching. During that time of withdrawal his understanding and resolve were tested by the devil. Jesus took strength and answers from Scripture and demonstrated his undeviating allegiance to God's word. Even then he did not go out teaching people, triumphant from his success of rebutting the devil, but remained in the desert looked after by the angels.

After a call, a person needs a time of nurturing, a time of waiting on God, a time of resting in his presence, a time of knowing God after the brightness of the vision has faded or the flood of feeling has ebbed. Visions are not sustainable and we cannot return to them. Ministry is exercised after we have reassessed normality. The world is a different place to us because the experience has happened. Spiritual experiences touch the whole person: thoughts, emotions, values, relationships. There may also be a physical healing or improvement in well-being. It is a form of resurrection: "get up, your faith has made you whole," where wholeness includes our entire way of responding to the world. A call is a great upheaval and the new person, the new servant of God, needs a period of "running in" after the intensity that wrought the change has subsided. You should be at peace with resting in the Lord and waiting on him and not feel compelled to rush into ministry until it is God's time for you to do so. Then you will be doing not just *your* best but *his* best in the ministry he has for you.

The Bible has many instances of calling and waiting. David the shepherd boy was anointed by Samuel well before his battle with Goliath—long enough to illustrate the difference between Samuel sending him into battle and David volunteering, having understood that as God's anointed he would fight in God's strength with certain success. It was still years before he was crowned as king.

Saul of Tarsus (Paul) underwent a dramatic conversion experience (Acts 9:1–19) and rushed into an enthusiastic preaching career but very soon got into trouble. He was sent home to Tarsus to wait safely on the Lord's better time; and when Barnabas perceived that time had come he went to Tarsus to fetch Saul and they spent a profitable year teaching in Antioch. During that peaceful period of ministry, the non-believers began to call disciples "Christians" for the first time. Paul's work did become very difficult and personally costly again, but by then he was fully affirmed in the blessings God was multiplying through his work. When persecutions were very heavy in Jerusalem and Rome, Paul's satellite churches among the Gentiles kept the faith alive. Christianity might not have survived if Paul had perished in his early arguments with the Hellenists (Acts 9:29).

Jesus preached with urgency about the kingdom of heaven being "at hand," and when he sent the Twelve (Luke 9:1–6) and then the seventy (Luke 10:1–12) out preaching and healing, it seemed under pressure of time. Time was short for his own life and he needed helpers to get the townsfolk and villagers ready to listen to him. The woman at the well in Samaria has a similar ministry of telling her neighbors about Jesus so that they come and hear him themselves and make the journey from secondhand to firsthand faith (John 4:39–42). When we think of the kingdom of heaven being "at hand," it is both imminent and near to us where we are in our individual lives. It means that the kingdom is right at our shoulder: if we turn around we shall be inside it. The kingdom is always so close that to become a servant is just to turn around and start walking toward Jesus. There is no ground to be made up before we can enter the kingdom; we simply turn our backs on all that is contrary to his will for us. When he is our King, we are inside his kingdom.

9. Preempting disappointment

The message given to Isaiah at Isaiah 6:9–13 seems strange. It is a denouncement like the message given to Samuel but was probably not his first pronouncement to the people. It reads like a summary of his forty years of prophecy. It is the disappointing outcome of all Isaiah's efforts written up as if that was how God had intended it to be. If we refer back to the idea of the holy remnant bringing glory to God then the prophecy comes true. The unholy have their chance to turn and repent but are deaf to God's call. They are purged away through invasions. In the historically different setting of Roman occupation, Jesus would not allow his disciples to call down holy wrath as fire from heaven on those who rejected him (Luke 9:54), but the strategy was to leave them alone and move on. The kingdom of God as Jesus preached it is not a territory but a matter of individual assent to God's rule. In our own sharings about God, Jesus's strategy is a good model to follow: sow the seeds and if they don't grow, move on. Some seed inevitably ends up on unsuitable ground; the miracle is that there is always a harvest in spite of the losses (Mark 4:3–20). Sometimes we are just the sower, and someone else will reap. Isaiah's call inspires us to remember the holiness of God, to keep returning to his presence and remember before whom we stand. When we remember God, our own life falls into perspective, and blessed again by his forgiveness we are renewed in our fitness and eagerness to be sent in his service. "Here am I, send me!"

Questions for reflection or group discussion

1. (a) In what ways are you able to make your faith "count" in your daily work and interactions—whether employed or not?
   (b) Do you conscientiously work as if for God? Could you do this?
2. (a) Do you have opportunities to talk about your Christian beliefs and activities with colleagues, neighbors, or family members who have lapsed from faith?
   (b) What could your church do to reach out to the lapsed? What resistances would it need to overcome, e.g. being out of the habit of churchgoing, guilt at falling away from faith, antipathy of family members, former "bad experience" of church?
3. (a) Do you feel "happy" and "productive" in your work—whether employed or not?
   (b) How could the idea of "being sent" help you to be more positive?

Additional Bible readings giving instances where people "recognize" Jesus, and experience the grief of a sinner and the salvation of his forgiveness

- Jesus at the house of Simon the Pharisee (Luke 7:36–50). Reflect on what Simon and the woman "see" in Jesus when they encounter him. Who is Jesus to them?
- The call of Simon Peter and his companions (Luke 5:1–11). The miraculous catch is evidence to Simon of who Jesus is; he is overcome with a

sense of sin. Jesus responds like a heavenly messenger saying, "Do not be afraid." Reflect on why Simon begs Jesus, "depart from me, for I am a sinful man." Is it because he "knows" you cannot see God and live (like Manoah and his wife), or because the presence of the Lord and of sin are painfully incompatible? The solutions are to separate from God or to be forgiven. Reflect on the consequences of both outcomes.

Summary of key themes
- The presence of God inspires awareness of sin. God wants to purify us so we are fit for his service. Forgiveness is complete. We do not carry around "forgiven sins" or "the sins of my past." They are gone.
- Our nearest mission field (after our household?) is the lapsed among our acquaintances.
- The success of our outreach hinges on people being able to "see the King"—to know the Lord for themselves.

Take-home message to think and pray about
- Like Isaiah, we may all have some mission to the lapsed whom we know. Our challenge is to encourage them back to the King they used to know, not to something they used to "do."

Prayer projects
- Pray for those people who are absent from church through a sense of sin or a fear of censure.
- Pray for an atmosphere of acceptance, forgiveness, and integration in your church building.
- Pray for chaplains working in industry, local hospitals, and prisons. Perhaps you can set up prayer

support for an individual chaplain and the cases they refer to you for prayer.
- Pray for the lapsed that they may hear the Lord calling them back into relationship with him.

Prayer

Mine eyes have seen the King, the Lord of Hosts.
Lord, grant me vision of your majesty,
sorrow to recoil from sin,
and a heart to embrace your mercy.
Lord, I am ready to serve you —
Here am I, send me.
Amen.

EPILOGUE

The aim of this book has been to affirm you in the reality of your relationship with God whether you are a child, a woman, or a man. The life of Jesus on earth assures us that God has personal business with each of us. Salvation is done on an individual basis, life by life by life. God wants to make himself known to you. If you are seeking a deeper relationship with him, be available to him, and may he bless you with indisputable knowledge of his constant presence and love.

www.ingramcontent.com/pod-product-compliance
Lightning Source LLC
Chambersburg PA
CBHW071220070526
44584CB00019B/3094